Journey To Ojà

Wálé Akíngbadé

Copyrighted Material

Journey to Ọjà

Copyright © 2025 by Wálé Akíngbadé / Think GTI Ltd.
All Rights Reserved

The moral right of the author has been asserted

No part of this publication may be reproduced, stored in a retrieval system or transmitted, in any form or by any means — electronic, mechanical, photocopying, recording or otherwise — without prior written permission from the publisher, except for the inclusion of brief quotations in a review.

For information about this title or to order other books and/or electronic media, contact the publisher:

Think GTI Ltd
distribution@thinkgti.com
www.thinkgti.com

ISBN-13: 978-1-0686543-5-0 / 979-8-2656439-1-9 (Hardcover edition)
ISBN-13: 978-1-0686543-4-3 (Paperback Edition)

A story about decision-making

Thanks to my editorial and production team for their creative input;
Canice Stephen (Editor) and Emmanuel Idoko (Illustrator)

Accompanied by an original music soundtrack.

scan me to listen

CONTENTS

7
HOME

15
PREPARATION

23
JOURNEY BEGINS

31
DISRESPECTFUL YOUNGER RIDER

43
SELFISH OLDER RIDER

53
JABARI'S REFLECTIONS

61
PITIFUL TREKKERS

69
THE MARKETPLACE

77
SEFU'S REFLECTIONS

85
POOR LOYAL HORSE

95
JOURNEY FROM OJÀ

101
HOME, SWEET HOME

chapter one
I

home

Once upon a time, a wealthy farmer named Obi lived in a remote village. At that time, renowned folk travelled on carriages pulled by horses, and most travelled on foot.

Obi owned several farm fields full of crops, fish ponds, poultry, and horses. On Obi's farm were gardens with exotic fruits and flowers seeded from foreign places he had travelled to.

Obi was a highly esteemed man. Although he inherited only a small farm from his father, he had increased his wealth significantly through hard work and a display of good character.

home

Both traits earned him the custom of many local aspirants and admiration amongst his friends.

At the time, Obi had two sons, Jabari and Sefu. Sefu was coming of age and would soon be in charge of cultivating the farm, taking over from his older brother, who had been working with his father as a merchant.

On the eve of Sefu's birthday, Obi asked Jabari to prepare to take his younger brother on a journey to Ojà, a town with a famous market where many merchants across the land come to transport and trade goods. The traders exchanged goods for cowries, the currency of trade in those days. Jabari was quite familiar with the road to Ojà and could travel there and back without guidance.

Every year since he was a teenager, Jabari followed in his father's footsteps, learning much about the family's business, meeting livestock suppliers, and purchasing and cultivating seeds needed to prepare for the coming seasons.

Obi had forged excellent relationships with merchants at Oja over the years, accepting promissory notes for more expensive goods — a form of 'I owe you' note to cover the difference for what was not paid for with cowries on the day. The notes represent a debt the buyers would repay to Obi within an agreed-upon timeframe.

The first time Jabari travelled to Ojà was 10 summers ago, when he was Sefu's age. So much had changed since then, yet much remained the same. The consistency brought about familiarity, helping Jabari to become a seasoned merchant in his own right.

It was time for Sefu's first trip, and Jabari was ready to lead his young brother.

home

chapter two

II

preparation

Sefu stayed up imagining what he would encounter on the journey with his brother: the numerous merchants, friendly foreigners, and colourful cultures that would make up significant parts of their adventure.

As they prepared to embark on their journey, Sefu showed signs of exhaustion. Unlike his older brother, it was the first time he would experience life outside his hometown.

The excitement kept him up all night as he had only ever known of the distant lands through stories Jabari told him.

Early that morning, as Obi reviewed what his sons would take with them, he asked Jabari to select a horse from the stable - one strong enough to carry heavy bags of resources needed for the journey.

"The road can be unpredictable," Obi said, "much of what you need you can find on your path, but a responsible traveller always ensures that the most important necessities are covered: a tent, some food and some water."

Jabari, ever the protective older brother, caught his young brother yawning as their father spoke. "I'll have to do a lot of walking early on, giving Sefu a chance to rest up." He added. Jabari knew his brother's excitement kept him up all night, and the younger sibling would need a steady start to their three-day journey.

Obi smiled and nodded with approval as Jabari proceeded to select a horse from the stable, and Sefu continued to prepare the bags for their journey.

The tent was carefully folded into a bag. Enough food for both brothers, water jugs, and hay to feed their horse were all in another bag. A pouch full of cowries to pay for the goods needed for the farm and a little extra for food.

Sefu ensured to pack his journal. He intended to capture every aspect of his new adventure, eager to fill the pages with stories to share with others in the future.

preparation 21

chapter three
III

journey begins

Journey to Ojà

With Jabari leading the way, Sefu settled into the saddle, feeling the warmth of the horse's body beneath him and the rough texture of the reins in his hands. His face, a mirror of his conflicting emotions, was a mix of exhilaration and fatigue.

It was a pleasant afternoon. The weather was not unbearably hot, but hot enough for Jabari to break a sweat.

Jabari began the story about the first time he had travelled with their father. "You were just an infant when Baba took me along on my first journey out of our town." He remembered, "...it was on a hot spring day like this one. Back then, it was not a three-day journey but one that lasted seven days each way because we travelled on foot and had to stop often."

Taking a long look over the hills, with their farm disappearing in the distance, Sefu felt exhausted at the thought of trekking. It wasn't long before he wondered how his older brother could easily navigate the woods. To Sefu, every view looked like the previous; it was impossible to tell which way to turn. Jabari had learnt to navigate the forest's seeming labyrinth from his father, using the sun, trees, and natural landmarks in the distance.

He reminded his brother about the story of the Iroko tree, which was Sefu's favourite story as a child, of an unusually tall tree that helped a lost girl find her way back to the village.

Explorers and surveyors would climb the tree to unveil new, more efficient travel routes. The tree stands in a town near Ojà. It remains distinctive due to its strong branches and has always been a significant landmark for navigators.

Very few speak of the Iroko today as it no longer bears fruit. Its roots still travel deep within the earth. Legends say the roots of Iroko trees still speak to lost travellers for those who know how to listen, resurfacing on remote paths to help them find their way home.

"Because of the Iroko tree," Jabari continued, reminding his brother, "we can now travel more efficiently with better routes."

"Ah, riding on a horse helps, too," added Sefu, with a mischievous grin as he sat comfortably in the saddle.

chapter four
IV

town one: disrespectful young rider

Journey to Ojà

After several hours of travelling through the wooded forest's trailing paths left by other travellers, they were starting to see people and could see the Iroko tree in the distance ahead.

The local people seemed friendly and greeted them cheerfully. Still, seeing an older man walking and a young boy sitting comfortably on a horse, they began to whisper amongst themselves, gesturing at the boy.

Sefu notices but ignores the gestures, as this is commonly done in his village whenever children see a stranger: they typically wave, point and make guesses about the traveller's origin.

However, these gestures felt very different. Jabari noticed on closer observation and became wary. Harsh stares and murmurs between the onlookers became more judgmental, with the townspeople displaying more animated gestures.

Later that afternoon, the two brothers found a spot to camp for the evening. Jabari sought answers about their experience, asking other travellers why he and his brother attracted so much unusual attention.

Jabari sought guidance from a kola nut merchant he'd noticed travelling along a similar path. "I have travelled through this route many times with my father and familiar with the attention of many onlookers, but this time is different. Even older people are raising their eyebrows and gesturing with disapproving looks," he asked as he took a measure of kola nuts from the merchant's stall.

"Well, isn't it obvious?" the merchant replied, "The locals perceive the young boy, I assume, to be your brother as disrespectful!"

"The culture of this land makes it clear. For a young boy to sit on a horse whilst a much older man walked is unheard of. If you continue this behaviour, you'll draw the wrong kind of attention, and people will speak ill of your brother."

So Jabari, realising the village's customs, thanked the merchant and asked his brother to step down to honour the local people's culture.

Jabari could tell by his attire that the merchant was renowned and respected in the village, much like their father.

From their conversation and subtle expressions, he understood that the merchant was genuinely interested in the well-being and safety of his customers, as well as in maintaining the integrity of the townspeople's customs.

The brothers would need a safe place to rest for the evening, so they asked the merchant for suggestions. He owned a cabin nearby and would have offered it to the brothers, but it was occupied by a guest who was spending the night. The cabin was situated in a safe part of the forest, just off the main path, and with plenty of camping space nearby, he suggested that the brothers set up their tent by the valley.

As the sun set, Jabari led the horse to the suggested spot, with Sefu closely following. With the dimly lit cabin further ahead on a hilltop, the brothers found a suitable place to pitch their tent. They ate, rested and prepared for the continuity of their journey the next day.

chapter five
V

town two: selfish older rider

The following day, the brothers discussed the previous day's events and the townspeople's negative comments about them. Jabari suggested adopting the village people's culture, where they spent the night. Sefu was well rested. He had ridden on the horse while his older brother walked through the harshest part of their journey.

Despite the criticism, the brothers had made a decision that suited them. Jabari would lead steadily on the horse while the young, agile Sefu would continue on foot for the day.

They soon arrived at the next village.

The inhabitants waved and clamoured from a distance, welcoming travellers and hordes of traders. Their friendliness wore off when they caught sight of the party of two brothers and their horse.

The whispers and finger-pointing became more prominent than in the previous village. Sefu caught the attention of an empathetic villager who offered some water, but only to Sefu and not his older brother.

Sefu was grateful for this gesture and offered some water to his older brother first. This act elicited a harsh response from the villagers as Jabari sipped. One

town two: selfish older rider

onlooker was outraged and couldn't help herself as she exclaimed, "Shame on you! How selfish of you to sit comfortably aloft on a saddle while you had this poor boy walking. Let him have a drink, will you!"

Shocked by this reaction, Sefu tried to explain to the woman, but another began to shout, and then another. The chorus of responses was so overwhelming that it left both travellers in awe. The villagers, too, were astonished. Their eyes were wide with disbelief as they witnessed the unprecedented scene before them.

In their culture, an older person, being more experienced and supposedly stronger, would be expected to be the one to walk, withstanding harsher conditions that the younger traveller ought not be subject to.

The local hecklers prevented the brothers from providing the full context of their decision to have the younger brother walk. There was no opportunity to explain what they had experienced the previous day.

With no patience to listen, the crowd began to get rowdy, so Jabari quickly dismounted instead of trying to reason with strangers.

His quick action prevented a riot, and the people soon dispersed one by one.

The brothers led the horse through an alley with only the load on its back to avoid the crowd of locals. They made a tent and spent the evening discussing the day's events, eating and feeding their horse. An early bedtime ensures they will earn enough rest for the third and final day of the journey.

chapter six
VI

Jabari's reflections

Early the following day, Sefu asked Jabari if he had a similar experience travelling with their father as they prepared for the day ahead.

It was one thing for Sefu to experience different cultures first-hand, but being judged so harshly by others was unexpected. It was even more frustrating that no one offered to educate them, seeing that the brothers were foreign to their culture.

"They didn't even try to understand our decisions," Sefu stated. "Have people always been this harsh with you on your travels? How did you manage to stay so calm?"

Jabari responded, "On my travels as a young man with Baba, I learned different lessons each time we were on the road. Mostly, it was more about perseverance and remembering routes to avoid bandits trying to steal whatever cowries or food we had."

"I also had to learn to keep up the pace — there was no slacking with Baba," Jabari remembered.

"When I started working and travelling with him, I had to learn quickly because slowing down was not an option. Could you imagine a seven-day journey turning out to be ten days?"

"'That only gave bandits more opportunity to find and rob us of what little profit we would make,' Baba would say."

They both chuckled, almost forgetting about their troubles with the angry villagers they had just evaded.

One thing about Obi's character is his confident, calm demeanour. Reflecting on this, Jabari added, "I also learned from Baba that you can not always control what's happening around you, but you can challenge yourself to control how you respond. That is how we play our part.

Journey to Oja

Rather than becoming a victim to the actions and criticism from those we encounter, we observe, learn, and adapt."

The journey had allowed Jabari to practise that lesson and now pass it on to his young brother.

chapter seven
VII

town three: pitiful walkers

Excited about the prospect of the final day's journey, Sefu would soon share a similar experience to that of Jabari and their father. Both brothers stuck to their decision of walking and allowing their horse to rest.

Several hours later, they arrived at the town of Ojà. It was nearing midday, and the sun was at its peak, making both sweat profusely. They approached the marketplace, with Jabari leading the horse and Sefu walking alongside him; both were visibly exhausted from the trek at high noon.

This time, no one criticised the travellers! Instead, the villagers looked curiously. Few quietly mocked them for their naivety, whilst the majority could not understand why a healthy half-loaded horse with a saddle was roaming without a rider while its seemingly exhausted owners were walking along.

"Come, look at these strange foreigners!" one exclaimed. "On such a hot day, imagine any sane person travelling on foot with a perfectly healthy and saddled horse."

As they walked on, they saw others coming out to stare at them, gesturing and laughing. The brothers heard someone pointing and saying in jest, "Look, there they go; the horse must be their master."

These gestures left Sefu embarrassed, but his brother encouraged him not to respond. He reminded Sefu of the lessons on observation and reaction. It was as crucial for Jabari to maintain his emotional stance internally. It was not about reacting to the jest but maintaining a healthy internal dialogue.

"What they are feeling and reacting to is based on their misunderstanding, not based on our naivety," said Jabari.

Understanding what his brother meant, Sefu turned his mind away from the noise and gestures and took a long, deep breath. "To the market. To the market." He repeated to himself.

chapter eight
VIII

the marketplace

Almost immediately, Sefu shifted his focus from what the onlookers had to say about him and his brother to what he thought of the moment and the beautiful scenes around him.

Ojà was now in sight, and Sefu's embarrassment became a curiosity richly fed with every gaze. The colours were more vibrant than he had imagined. Traders of seeds, silk, spices, precious metals, handicrafts, paintings, livestock and fruits of all kinds camped in clusters and traded among themselves.

Sefu took in the vibrant scenes,

the marketplace

watching traders greet Jabari as the brothers walked around Ojà, going from stall to stall to negotiate and make deals with merchants.

He observed curiously as Jabari made arrangements to have stocks of grain, eggs, and milk collected from their farm, and merchants made deposits in the form of cowries and seeds. For those who could not pay the full amount on the day, promissory notes were signed and given to Jabari.

Sefu felt a gleeful pride when Jabari introduced him to merchants as his young brother. Merchants would then ask about their father's well-being with reverence. Obi was renowned for a highly esteemed reputation. His character traits earned his sons more respect and trust at Ojà.

Jabari took a bite from one of the exchanged fruits: a ripe, red rose apple, exposing the seeds on the inside. A satisfied Jabari chewed with glee, soaking up the juices. He then shared the remnant with Sefu and explained the fruit's value to his young brother.

"From just one seed from this fruit, we can grow a tree full of fruit, from which we could eventually plant a row

of trees. So enjoy the fruit, but never to the extent that you consume the seeds. Always be mindful of saving them for planting." Attentive to his brother's dealings, Sefu, too, chewed with satisfaction as he pondered all he had learned on the journey.

From navigating travel routes using nature's landmarks and the Iroko tree to the cultures of each town they rode through, he understood the importance of relationships with other merchants and the value of a reputable character.

chapter nine

IX

Sefu's reflection

Sefu imagined starting a garden of his own on a small plot back home, where he would plant those seeds. He was excited to learn and keen to start the cultivation process.

Jabari handed Sefu the promissory notes from the merchants to keep safe. He tucked them in his pouch and grabbed his journal to add one more entry. Sefu was very proud of all the notes and sketches he had done so far of his first journey to Ojà.

In his journal, Sefu wrote down all the insights and details on a series of pages in a section titled "My First Journey with Jabari." On preparation, Sefu learnt to

1. Plan and properly pack, "proper preparation is half the journey," Sefu recalled his father's words.

2. Travel light, but ensure one has enough of the most valuable resources.

3. Navigate unfamiliar routes using natural resources, like the sun and trees; these elements are always present and universally trustworthy.

4. Pause when necessary; take time out for rest and recovery.

Sefu also made the following notes from the people he encountered.

5. There are times to speak to ask essential questions, listen and understand others' perspectives.

6. There are times to be silent and observant, not to engage in conversations that could stir strife.

7. There are times to act, confronting a situation to find a resolution.

8. There are times to stay idle, waiting for the dust of chaos to settle on its own accord.

From the marketplace at Ojà, he learnt;

9. To be flexible.

10. To negotiate fairly on every deal, never to compromise his integrity. After all, what is a man's worth when his reputation is without merit?

11. To seek value in places where others may not readily notice.

12. It is essential to see a single seed as more than surplus inside the fruit. Acknowledge its potential and the work required for its transformation.

chapter ten

X

poor loyal horse

Sefu learned that the right thing to do depends on the time and situation. He knows to remain calm and to be careful when reacting to criticism. Clarifying anything misunderstood helps, because emotional reactions can lead to undesired outcomes like the riot Jabari quelled before kicking off.

It was now evening, and the market at Ojà had started to shut down. Merchants with loaded carts had begun to finalise deals as they prepared for closure. With a couple of pouches of cowries, a stack of promissory notes and a small sack of fruits, the brothers made a tent for the evening and planned the journey home early the next morning.

Jabari thoroughly enjoyed his brother's company, grateful for their father's instruction to take Sefu along. For the days ahead, he would let Sefu lead the way home and make all the significant decisions.

Sefu was thrilled! With little contemplation, he suggested, "Why don't we ride the horse home together!" They hadn't done that on the journey towards Ojà. After all, Sefu thought, there was little to carry home. The people along the way who had criticised them, displeased with either or both of them walking, would have nothing negative to say to the brothers.

Jabari agreed. He had chosen this particular horse because it was one of the larger and stronger horses in their father's stable. He also brought a saddle and tack suitable for double riding, which was also used to carry the goods they brought to Ojà.

Sefu did not expect the response he got from onlookers. The brothers barely made it out of Ojà before the criticisms began. "Both of you on this poor animal!" exclaimed one passer-by, unaware of the strength and tolerance of their horse.

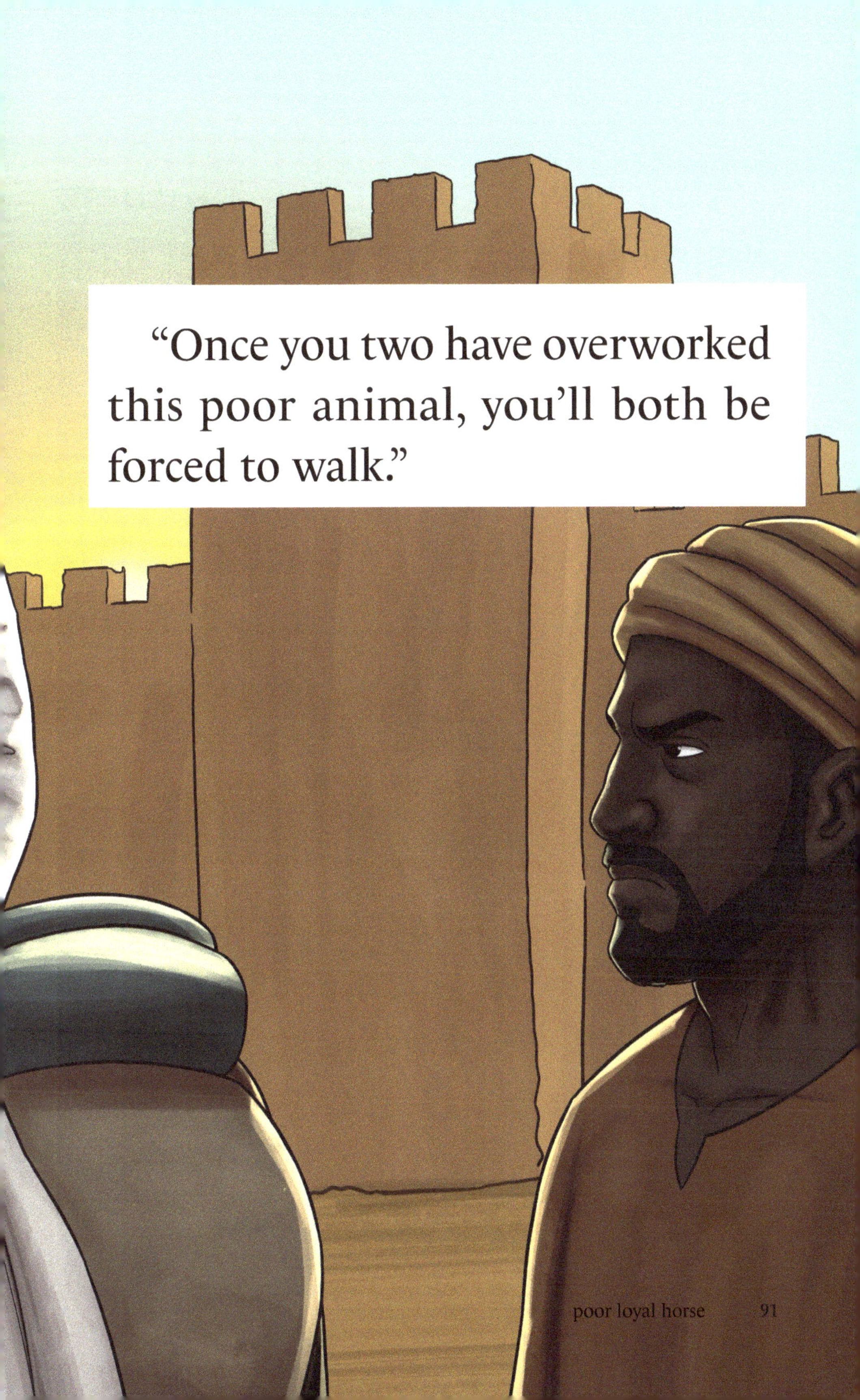

“Once you two have overworked this poor animal, you’ll both be forced to walk.”

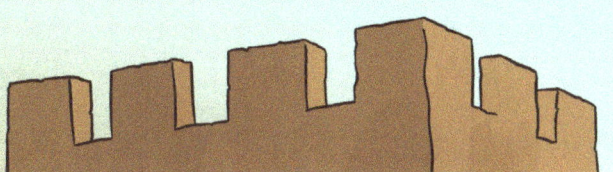

Another stared at the brothers disapprovingly as they rode past him, his carriage of goods pulled by two horses.

Sefu had thought through his plan and had decided to do what was most suitable for himself, his brother, and their horse, but observers' voices of disapproval continued to echo.

He confided in his older brother, "Regardless of what we do, it seems there will always be voices who criticise us. You know what?" Sefu added. "If it's a choice between living with my decision and worrying about others' judgment, it's obvious which I'd pick."

Jabari laughed, agreeing with his brother. "Wisely spoken, Sefu. There might come a time when you've made the best decision in a situation, but a different perspective could raise unfounded doubts, causing you to hesitate or question yourself." Jabari added.

"You may discuss alternative options with someone knowledgeable and trustworthy. When you find peace with your decision, take action and remember you do not have to justify it to strangers."

chapter eleven

XI

the journey home

Jabari continued imparting advice to his brother as they rode on the back of their robust and capable horse, "The true measure of peace is when a decision is aligned with your deepest values. Like your thoughts and emotions, this peace is very personal and impossible to share with others in its purest form."

"Few will seek to understand your reasons and engage in meaningful dialogue, and you will learn from them. Others will criticise without trying to understand you - this is a moment they will soon forget, and so should you."

The brothers could see their home in the distance, but their focus was much closer: the next step, the comfort of each other's company and the confidence to make decisions that suited them.

From the moment they decided to embark on the journey, they knew the road ahead would prepare them for unique experiences and challenges.

They came to realise that there was no need to overthink past or future interactions, because the cost of missing all the beauty and value of present moments was too great.

Besides focusing solely on the destination, it is essential to stop often, take a breath and take in the view!

For the first time on the journey, Sefu noticed how beautiful the sky looked: a beautiful gradient on the horizon painted next to a fading sunset! He could hear the rustling of leaves in the woods provoked by soft, random breezes. Soothing sounds from birds nested above them echoed.

At that very moment, everything surrounding their path became unique and precious.

chapter twelve
XII

home, sweet home

Sefu knows that the road will differ between this journey and the next. The world will still be here, but the people will change. Some strangers will become friends, bringing new ideas to life and doubtful decisions to criticise.

Everything else left to do, based on his experience, is to follow his path with one constant: to possess the ability to observe and adapt. The journey home had profoundly transformed Sefu in ways he was only beginning to comprehend.

As they neared the familiar sight of their father's farm, he was struck by the

transformation of the landscape. The once ordinary scenery now shimmered with new hues and contours, a testament to the transformative power of their journey.

Months drifted by, and the seeds of wisdom sown during the journey to Ojà had begun to blossom in Sefu's life. His interactions with fellow villagers, decisions on his father's farm, and his overall perspective were all shaped by the lessons he learned on the road to Ojà.

One day, as Sefu and his brother

stood amidst the rose apple trees that now adorned his garden, he couldn't help but marvel at the beauty that sprouted from his snack.

The very trees that began as seeds from their journey had flourished into a symbol of growth and resilience. Obi, observing his son from a distance, approached with a knowing smile. "The journey never truly ends, Sefu; it merely paves the way for new beginnings."

Each season brought new experiences, along with winds of change. The natural elements that guided Obi's sons to Ojà also led them towards a

Journey to Ojà

deeper understanding of life's intricate paths.

And so, in the shade of the rose apple trees, Sefu embraced the beauty of the present moment. He realised that each step taken on the journey to Ojà had paved the way for a lifetime of continuous growth.

Standing in awe of the beauty of being truly present, Sefu finally understood he would not have reached this point without the culmination of all the precious past footsteps of his journey.

Closing Thoughts

The journey towards growth and self-actualisation involves several significant and transformative decision points, and it's natural to feel judged by others. However, it's essential to remember that their judgments reflect a projection of their perceptions and self-assessment. When we face criticism, we must accept that it is often veiled projections of the critic's inner reflections, and it is not our responsibility. Instead, we must be patient and cautious and seek understanding before responding.

To appreciate our progress, we must embrace life's journey, which is full of continuous transformation and unique experiences that offer perpetual growth. Getting caught up in the past or future is easy, but reflecting on our growth can help us replenish our confidence, foster gratitude, and ignite inspiration.

The transient nature of existence imbues each moment with significance and value. Recognising this short-lived beauty can infuse our lives with preciousness, encouraging us to appreciate the present moment. We must learn to be empathetic to ourselves and others as we navigate life's journey, as it's not always easy. By practising empathy for ourselves and others, we can lead a more fulfilling life.